DESTINY
DECISIONS

DAN HOOPER

ISBN: 0-9793192-0-X
978-0-9793192-0-4

Published by

LIFEBRIDGE
BOOKS
P.O. BOX 49428
CHARLOTTE, NC 28277

Printed in the United States of America.

DEDICATION AND ACKNOWLEDGMENTS

*First and foremost I want to thank my Savior,
my Lord and my closest friend. Thank you for
saving me at the age of 12 and for taking me on a
journey that has made living this life an exciting,
challenging and blessed ride.*

*Thank you Anna for making me smile.
Your sweet, fun loving heart and laughter for life
and family has caused me to slow down and really
appreciate the important simple things in life.*

*Dan, my son: You have enriched my life in more
ways than I could ever explain. The anointing our
God has placed on you, your leadership and love for
Him and His people truly inspires me all over
again. I love doing His work with you.*

*Mindi, my daughter. I love your zeal for life
and your passion for worshiping The Father.
You are a beautiful example of living
the resilient life God had in mind.*

*The People of Fellowship Church: Anna and
I have never known any other group of God's
people who are so generous, kind and enthusiastic
for Him. Thank you for staying with us through
all the changes and living out His adventure
that has been Fellowship Church.*

CONTENTS

INTRODUCTION

Life comes down to two main questions: Where are you going to spend eternity when you die and how are you going to spend the days you have left until that day arrives?

Many of the people I know have settled the first question by asking Jesus into their heart—and by doing so they have made Him the most important person in their life, loving Him with all of their heart, mind, soul and spirit. However, the problem arises with the realization their existence really doesn't look much different from the time before they were saved.

Salvation through Christ changed their eternal destination, but there are some key decisions we still have to make to alter the way we live while we are here on earth. These decisions and how to make them are the driving force behind this book.

Many people are stuck in the same rut year after year. Their relationships are good but not really great, their finances are almost enough to scrape by on, but not sufficient to do the things they always wanted to do and their overall joy and happiness level does not match up with the way they have always hoped and dreamed. It's time to get "unstuck" and get your life going again.

This book will give you God's principles for living. It will also present the answers you need to make the best decisions possible to get you up and going in the right direction. God never meant for you to fail or to remain trapped in the same dull, unfulfilled way day after day.

No matter where you have been or what you have done, God wants to take you on a wonderful adventure and make every area of your journey more fulfilling. So it's time to put your life in orbit by making prayerful, wise decisions—and the first one you need to make is to read on!

– Dan Hooper

CHAPTER ONE

ANYWHERE BUT BACKWARDS

It doesn't make any sense, does it? Why keep doing life the way you've been doing it when your present routine is not bringing you the desired results? If you want your world to be better, it starts simply by making better decisions!

Let me tell you about Jim.

It only took me about ten minutes to figure out where this guy was going: backwards! Another failed relationship, another lonely stage of life and more financial loss. Instead of moving forward, Jim keeps making the same negative choices, and as a result, the outcome is very similar to what he has always experienced: disappointment, loneliness and loss.

Your existence on this planet today is a sum total of the decisions you have made. Whether they were good ones or bad, you are on the rung of life's ladder right now as a direct result of your choices. The exciting news is that you can alter your present circumstances and change the direction of your future.

Jim resembles so many who find themselves repeating their past or feeling trapped in the present with little hope of the future ever really turning out the way they dreamed. With divorce papers in hand and another wife and child moving to another state, this small business owner whose vibrant zeal for living was now broken before me. Jim had made some horrible decisions. No, not with another woman, but with the wife he had been married to for the past fifteen years. He decided to "do life" and love without God. He tried to build a business and a family on his own, under his personal strength and wisdom, and he failed miserably.

NO MORE REPETITION

Anytime you really take a close look at God's people in the Bible, you will see how they are either moving forward or they are *preparing* to move ahead.

If you ever read of them languishing in one place or just circling in a desert, it is usually because they have failed to listen and obey the Almighty. If we are experiencing the same thing over and over again, we are not leading a productive or exciting life, just repeating an old used one. This means we have not heard or followed the commands of the One who made and created us for success. The God who formed you to experience an adventure in partnership with Him did not intend for you to only repeat the same thing time after time, rather to keep you moving forward in your love, relationships and finances —rising to the next level.

Repetitive living doesn't require a lot of faith, it just takes a good memory!

Know Where You're Climbing

I once heard a life application illustration many years ago that I have never forgotten. Zig Ziglar asked, "What if you were to spend your whole life climbing the ladder, and toward the end of your climb you get somewhere close to the top only to find out that it was leaning against the wrong building?"

11

Perhaps you are exhausting yourself by taking steps in a relationship which is headed in the wrong direction. However, you are so busy and focused in the activity of it all that you don't realize until it is too late, all your effort in advancement is actually taking you backwards.

Someday, many years into the process, you will need to stop, climb back down, and start all over again with the life you have left. This is not only true in relationships, but is also prevalent in so many other areas.

So what do you say we just stop here and now —and make sure our ladder isn't propped up against the wrong building. Before engaging in anymore exhausting steps to reach where we think we are headed, let's pause and find out if we have made the right decision to begin with.

THERE'S A REASON

First, you must find the answer to this all important question: "Why are you here?"

Why are you on this planet right now at your age and in this place in time? Why did God create you?

Let's see what the Scripture has to say:

> *For you created my inmost being; you knit*
> *me together in my mother's womb. I praise you*
> *because I am fearfully and wonderfully made; your*
> *works are wonderful, I know that full well.*
> —PSALM 139:13-14 NIV

WHY AM I HERE?

I want to help you answer this question by giving you five things God *didn't* create you to be:

1. *You are not here so you can be lonely.*

God proclaimed in the very beginning of time that is was not a healthy thing for anyone to exist in a state of loneliness.

> *The Lord God said,*
> *"It is not good for man to be alone."*
> — GENESIS 2:18

13

Since God is the One who created us in the first place it only makes sense to listen to Him when it comes to how we are supposed to live on His earth. So, if you are existing by yourself, this is not what the Lord had in mind.

Two are better than one, because they
have a good return for their work: If one falls
down, his friend can help him up. But pity the man
who falls and has no one to help him up!
– ECCLESIASTES 4:9-10 NIV

About one third of all the people who come to our church each week are single adults. Of course, you don't have to be single to be lonely. There are countless numbers of men and woman in marriage relationships who go through suspended times of loneliness, but for the sake of understanding the issue of "doing life alone" and not by personal choice, I want to give you some answers. I have found there are several reasons most people find themselves being very lonely:

AN OVERLY GUARDED HEART

If you are past the age of twenty, you have probably been hurt at one time or another by the betrayal of a trusted friend. It is at this point when you have a decision to make—to love and trust again or to erect a wall around your heart to keep others away.

When you decide to build such a barrier, your very demeanor will tell others you are unapproachable. Even though deep down you would love to resume dating, or just be in a close relationship again, your decision to not forgive those in your past or to not allow yourself to be vulnerable will isolate you from the new friends God would love you to meet.

POOR PEOPLE SKILLS

I am convinced most individuals who have low relational skills probably don't realize this. However, those of us who are around them pick up on it very quickly. When a person is lacking in this area they will usually be talking about themselves rather than showing interest in those around them. They rarely, if ever, build up others by showing genuine concern for the people they meet. They are often rude, negative,

15

inconsiderate and lack simple social etiquette. When describing this type of individual who usually stands just outside of your circle, you would never use words like, "giving" or "generous."

The good news is that people skills can be learned and applied to reverse a secluded lifestyle.

Failure to Take Initiative

Many people who experience a lonely existence are inwardly waiting for someone to come along and change the situation. These can be individuals who are aggressive when it comes to their work or daily activities, however, when it involves friendships or dating they seem to be stuck in the slow lane. If only I could open up a live video feed into my office just for the last two years and let you watch and listen to the number of single adults who would love to have a person to just eat a meal with and talk to, but who will not take the initiative themselves to approach another person!

Of course, the fear of rejection plays a huge role in their passive decision, even though they are often very sharp people. These are men and women who almost anyone would enjoy being involved in a friendship with, yet sadly, they sit back and wait for a person who in reality is also sitting back and waiting! They can't seem to realize that in every other area, where they are more successful, they are the ones who are aggressively going after it.

For God did not give us the spirit of timidity, but a spirit of power, of love and of self discipline.
– 2 TIMOTHY 1:7

This leads us to another example of what God did *not* create us to be:

2. You are not here so you can be fearful.

I was speaking with a woman who has been a Christian for many years and asked her. "How are things going?"

She replied, "Not very good these days—so I spend most of my time worrying and praying."

Why would we want to do both? If we are just going to worry about things, why pray? And if we are really going to pray over them, why worry?

When we talk to the God of this universe concerning issues or challenges in our lives and truly turn them over to Him, the only question remaining is, "What does God want us to do?" And "What will His part be in the process?"

Worry is not an activity God intended for His people to waste their time on. Even more, it has the potential of robbing us from enjoying the adventure the Lord has planned.

3. You are not here to play it safe.

God's children have always had a history of advancement. We have been forward-moving, risk-taking men and women of faith—a people who could visualize before they could actually see. These are individuals who can see by faith in their minds eye what they would soon see in the physical as a result of their belief and trust in God. Besides, haven't you found that playing it safe is boring and predictable? Isn't this what almost everyone is doing?

I would dare say that in your heart of hearts God has placed a passion, a dream you are supposed to strive for that still visits your thinking from time to time. I'm talking about an adventure which is way out of your comfort zone, one you couldn't do in your own ability or resources. Something only God would be able to make happen.

And therein lies your quest—to make the decision to partner with the Lord for a God-size dream. It could be starting your own business, making an investment or beginning a new relationship, but the very thought of it means God is going to have to intervene or this objective will certainly fail. You could go for it, or you can just take the path most people choose and play it safe. How boring!

4. You are not here to barely get by.

I'm not the kind of person who believes it is God's will for everyone to be rich, but I do not believe it is His intention for anyone to starve either. Over and over again in His Word we see God teaching us how we can prosper.

The word "prosper" means to flourish or thrive. This indicates that prospering is not just about having more money, but it can also include your relationships and other endeavors being more successful. Take a look at the following verse:

The Lord was with Joseph and he prospered.
– GENESIS 39:2 NIV

Think about this for a moment. What else was going to happen when the Lord was with Joseph? Could it have read that the Lord was with him or on his side and he failed miserably and lost it all? No, when God is with you, in the long run you can't do anything else but prosper.

This doesn't mean you will not go through times of testing, even loss. But if you stay faithful, learning and growing, you will thrive and prosper in His presence.

The Lord commanded us to obey all these decrees and to fear the Lord our God, so that we might always prosper and be kept alive, as is the case today.
– DEUTERONOMY 6:24 NIV

Obey and respect—to treat our Lord the way He is supposed to be treated—are the key ingredients to knowing abundance. However, as in any great relationship there must always be trust. Our God wants you to totally have faith and confidence in Him, to believe what He says by living the way He tells us to.

What if you finally make this decision? What if you decide that from this moment forward you are going to do everything God's way? What would be the outcome?

A greedy man stirs up dissension,
but he who trusts in the Lord will prosper.
– PROVERBS 28:25 NIV

You don't have to settle for being broke and living paycheck to paycheck just because your parents may have lived that way. With God's help you can break the cycle and live according to His design and purpose.

"For I know the plans I have for you," declares
the Lord, "plans to prosper you and not to harm you,
plans to give you hope and a future."
– JEREMIAH 29:11 NIV

I can guarantee that God *does* have the best blueprint for your future, so decide here and now that you are going to stop listening to what everyone else has spoken over you and start to simply trust Him and live according to His plans and purposes for you.

5. You are not here so you can be miserable.

Living is not always going to be easy—and for one simple reason: this is not heaven. The Lord tells us that on this earth we will have trouble, sorrow and will experience seasons of pain, grief and loss. But these times are just temporary. We know we are going to encounter difficulties, yet this does not mean we have to become discouraged or settle for disappointment.

I have told you these things, so that in me you may have peace. In this world you will have trouble. But take heart! I have overcome the world.
– JOHN 16: 33 NIV

I love how the Amplified Bible explains this:

*In the world you have tribulation and trials and
distress and frustration; but be of good cheer [take
courage; be confident, certain, undaunted]! For I have
overcome the world. [I have deprived it of power to
harm you and have conquered it for you.]*

Even in the midst of our problems, we are to still live as conquerors and exhibit the courage to have a joy-filled, confident, abundant life. Jesus tells us His purpose in coming to earth was not only to give us a perfect eternal home in heaven, but to also offer us His favor right now.

*The thief comes only in order to steal and kill and
destroy. I came that they may have and enjoy life, and
have it in abundance (to the full, till it overflows).*
– JOHN 10:10 AMP

This sounds like a pretty good way to exist—in joy and abundance as opposed to misery and poverty.

GET GOING AGAIN!

Back to Jim. It was obvious to me that day how

miserable he truly was. His life, family and marriage was anything other than what Jesus described in the above passage, but he felt trapped and unable to decide what to do in order to make things different. By his own admission, Jim was just repeating the same mistakes, wasting years and continuing in the same vicious cycle. We will talk about him a little more later.

So if you are feeling stuck in a place of loneliness, fear, border-line poverty, boredom or lacking true excitement and joy, isn't time to *get your life going again?*

In the next chapter we are going to discover the real reason God placed you here. Then you can decide if you want to live out His promises or just keep things as they have been. I hope you will make the right choice, because this next decision is about to determine your destiny!

CHAPTER TWO

WHAT WILL YOU DO WITH THE LIFE YOU HAVE LEFT?

J im looked a little puzzled when I asked him if he had been taking his family to church on the weekends. This was an extremely busy business owner with lots of clients and a work schedule where the idea of punching a time clock in and out had been no where in his history.

"Church?" he answered. "I haven't been attending. I used to go several years back, but I haven't been in a church for years."

As a minister, I will be the first to tell you that just

adding a church service once or twice a week to your agenda is certainly not the only answer for fixing all of life's problems, but his reply gave me further insight to the amount of attention he had or not been giving to the spiritual needs of his now-estranged family.

A wife for fifteen years and an eight-year-old son had never seen their dad give any priority to relying on God. The result was, they were struggling, trying to hold onto their fractured family.

What Jim longed for is what most of us desire, a mutually satisfying, fulfilling and fun marriage, children who love and respect him and a workplace that brings enjoyment and purpose. But how does a person find all these things without the help of our Creator. The answer is easy—you don't!

TRUE HAPPINESS?

Even if you were to attain wealth, fame and influential power you will soon discover, like most people do, an empty feeling that something is missing. Where is the vital personal connection with the One who made you?

In a recent interview with Brad Pitt, *Rolling Stone*

Magazine asked him if obtaining all his success had caused him to find true happiness and meaning in life. His answer: *"If you ask me, I say toss all of this, we gotta find something else. The emphasis now is on success and personal gain. I'm sitting in it and I'm telling you that's not it. I'm the guy who has everything, I know, but I'm telling you, once you have everything then you're just left with yourself. It doesn't help you sleep any better and you don't wake up any better off because of it."*

In order for anyone to experience a meaningful existence they must begin to comprehend why they are here in the first place. A full understanding of this will contribute so many wonderful additions for "doing life" better.

UNCONDITIONAL LOVE

I believe there are only two real reasons why you are alive today, and when you fully grasp them you will also find the motivation and inspiration you need to make changes in every other area that needs to be made new.

Reason #1: You are here because God loves you.

He created you to love and more than anything else He wants you to try to understand how much. For it is only by realizing how deeply the Father cares for you that you will be able to really start living. Notice what the apostle Paul says concerning God's unconditional love:

> Then Christ will make his home in your
> hearts as you trust in him. Your roots will grow
> down into God's love and keep you strong. And
> may you have the power to understand, as all God's
> people should, how wide, how long, how high, and
> how deep his love is. May you experience the love of
> Christ, though it is too great to understand fully. Then
> you will be made complete with all the fullness
> of life and power that comes from God.
>
> — EPHESIANS 3:17-19

When will you be made complete with all the fullness of life and power? When you begin to know how much you are cherished by the Creator. It changes everything. Just take a look at some of the ways a fuller understanding of His love for you will affect your life:

First: You will stop living with so much personal guilt.

God longs to forgive your sins. He easily does this because of His continual love for you. He is not mad or upset—and if you will just talk to Him and stop trying to hide your failings, the Lord will forgive and treat you as if that sin had never happened. He does not want there to be any distance or separation between you.

> *But if we confess our sins to him, he is faithful and just to forgive us our sins and to cleanse us from all wickedness.*
> – 1 JOHN 1:9

Second: You will walk with confidence.

When you know without a shadow of doubt how much you are treasured by the Most High God, you will start to walk and project yourself with strength and confidence. I'm not referring to a spirit of arrogance. I am talking about an inner poise that gives you a demeanor of being a winner. You don't have to continue with uncertainty regarding where you came from and who you belong too. God has claimed you for His very own and you no longer have to approach the world with an air of timidity or fear. His love gives you a sense of belonging and a holy boldness.

The wicked run away when no one is chasing them, but the godly are as bold as lions.

– PROVERBS 28:1

This new, positive attitude will change the way you perform your work, decrease the amount of time you spend worrying and brighten your outlook for the future. Confident living is strong and attractive and it makes others around you want to know what really caused the transformation. It is so appealing to those who are lost that our enemy (Satan) tries to sabotage your knowledge of God's love anyway he can.

One of the most effective methods the devil uses

to subvert a person from really understanding the Father's love is through God's own representatives.

"HERE WE GO AGAIN!"

Immediately after Jim told me he no longer went to church, he followed up with his reason for why. "I attended a parochial Catholic School when I was a child."

I thought to myself, "Here we go again. I'm about to hear another 'mean nun' story!"

Then he continued, "There was this nun who used to belittle and tell me how stupid I was on a regular basis. She even met with my parents, telling them I didn't have the capacity to learn like the other children. That Nun damaged me as a small boy and..."

Well, I'm sure you know the rest of the story. He stopped attending a House of God until he was in his young twenties when he started to attend a Baptist church. I thought to myself, "Oh, here we go again. A Baptist church story!"

He further added, "I was teaching a seventh grade boys class when someone asked me if I had ever been divorced. When I told them I had, they took away my class and kicked me out of the congregation."

Well I'm more then certain Jim exaggerated the details at least a little, but you should have seen the look on his face when my response to the two alleged acts of being targeted by so-called Christians was simply, "So? What does any of that have to do with your God?"

I think it was the first time he had ever seriously thought about the question. I asked Jim, "How does anything that a person who is supposed to be representing God have anything to do with you and your personal relationship with Him? God didn't call you stupid or banish you from His church or hurt you in anyway. So why did you stop talking to Him? Why didn't you look for a church were you could learn more about the Lord and grow, serve, and give back to Him?

I think he was in shock and I saw a light turn on in his thinking. "I guess it had nothing to do with God," he responded.

"That's right," I agreed, "absolutely nothing."

WHO IS TO BLAME?

I then asked him, "What if you had an employee

who didn't present your company in its best light to your clients. Are you personally to blame for his misrepresentation? Is the individual who lacked the ability to communicate at fault?"

He answered, "The employee, of course."

Then I asked, "Why would you think that God's employees are any different?"

People who serve the Lord and call themselves His children mess up all the time. It has absolutely nothing to do with God's goodness. It's *them* who are misrepresenting, mean spirited or just plain wrong, not the Lord. However, this doesn't change the fact God loves us and has never hurt us in any way. We must be able to separate the Lord from everyone else and accept His divine embrace for ourselves.

Third: You will want to experience more of His love.

Finally, when you start to truly comprehend the amount of care and concern your Father has for you, you will want to draw into a close and very personal relationship with Him. You will begin to realize that no one on this planet will be able to love you to that extent—not just now, but for eternity.

With some people, the more you get to know them, the less you want to be around them! With our heavenly Father it is just the opposite. He knows our innermost secrets, yet He will never abandon us because of our shortcomings.

> Be strong and courageous. Do not be afraid or terrified because of them, for the Lord your God goes with you; he will never leave you nor forsake you.
> — DEUTERONOMY 31:6 NIV

Desiring to draw closer to the Lord leads us to the second reason why you have been placed on this earth:

Reason # 2: You are here to love God back.

When Jesus was asked by His disciples what was the most significant thing we were to remember and do with our life, His answer was insightful. He didn't give a list of do's and don'ts, but instead issued a command that makes anyone who hears it stand in awe of an Almighty God who just wants His children to love Him back:

> *He asked him, "Of all the commandments,*
> *which is the most important?" "The most important*
> *one," answered Jesus, "is this: 'Hear, O Israel, the*
> *Lord our God, the Lord is one. Love the Lord your*
> *God with all your heart and with all your soul and with*
> *all your mind and with all your strength.'"*
> — MARK 12:28-29 NIV

God simply desires for you to love Him in return. Wow! More than anything else you can do for Him, any sacrifice you may make or any amount of money you could give, God just wants you to love Him more than anyone or anything else.

How is this demonstrated? Loving God with all your heart, soul, mind and strength is not shown by sitting around in a prayer meeting 24-hours a day. It involves including Him in every aspect of your existence.

If you are married and love your wife, do you spend every waking moment waiting for the chance to tell her you love her over and over again? No, together you experience fun and laughter, sorrow and grief, good times and bad with the person you love and are committed to.

The same is true with God. When you care for Him the way He wants you to, you include Him in every thought and action. This is an "All Out," fully committed kind of love. And it is what the Lord is looking for from you.

For the eyes of the Lord range throughout the earth to strengthen those whose hearts are fully committed to him.
– 2 CHRONICLES 16:9 NIV

Think about it for a moment. God is searching for the person who He can get behind and totally affirm. One translation says He is looking for someone "He can show Himself strong on their behalf."

The criteria for receiving this level of "God backing" is an unfaltering love for Him. This is my desire and I pray it is yours as well: to live with a heart fully committed to God and experience the strong support of the Lord in every corner of my life.

This concept of reciprocating God's love is personal and powerful—and it all begins by accepting His Son Jesus as your Savior. God loved you so much that He allowed Jesus to die for you. You accept this amazing *un-earnable* gift by asking Christ to save you and make a commitment to live with Him.

> *Everyone who calls on the*
> *name of the Lord will be saved.*
> – ROMANS 10:13 NIV

> *Salvation is found in no one else, for*
> *there is no other name under heaven given to*
> *men by which we must be saved.*
> – ACTS 4:12 NIV

Once you have connected with Jesus, you have made the single greatest decision you will ever make. Now you are ready to settle this question: What will you do with the life you have left?

Whether you have many years or only a short time remaining on this earth, what truly matters is how you are going to live from this day forward.

37

Your past no longer matters. The decision you have to make concerns today and tomorrow. In the next three chapters you will find the biblical principles for altering any area of your walk that needs to be redirected. If you don't like the way your life is going, there is only one thing to do—change course!

CHAPTER THREE

CHANGE!

A llow me to repeat the final words of the previous chapter: If you don't like the way your life is going, there is only one thing to do—change course!

Stop complaining about your present situation, quit repeating your same mistakes, and decide to do things in a new way. Partner with Almighty God and make things happen.

I pray you have already settled life's biggest question, "Where am I going from here? Where will I spend eternity?"

If you have asked Jesus to be your Savior, you have made a destination change from spending eternity in hell to being assured of an everlasting home in heaven. Congratulations! It is the smartest decision you will ever make.

Keep asking yourself, "How do I want to spend the time I have left on earth before I get to Heaven? This is your choice, and one which has to be made in order to experience the best life possible.

You changed your destination by making a salvation decision, now you can impact the rest of your days with a divine transformation of your mind. Reordering the way you think will alter everything else.

THREE INGREDIENTS

I want to give you a formula from God's Word you can use when you want to experience something new—and make it permanent:

Change   Construct   Complete

We will address the first ingredient—*change*—in this chapter, and focus on the remaining two later.

Whether your marriage desperately needs to be revitalized, your career seems to have hit a brick wall and is going nowhere, or you just need to lose a few pounds, these principles from God's Word all deal with becoming a better you. How you spend your future is entirely up to you. No one else can make this decision. So if you're ready to start moving in the direction you have always dreamed of, it begins with *changing* the way you think.

> *Don't copy the behavior and customs of*
> *this world, but let God transform you into a*
> *new person <u>by changing the way you think</u>. Then*
> *you will learn to know God's will for you,*
> *which is good and pleasing and perfect.*
> – ROMANS 12:2

> *Do not be conformed to this world*
> *(this age), [fashioned after and adapted to its*
> *external, superficial customs], but be transformed*
> *(changed) by the [entire] renewal of your mind*
> *[by its new ideals and its new attitude].*
> – AMPLIFIED VERSION

Many who have accepted Jesus as their Lord still continue living much the same way they were before their conversion. Their family, finances and overall existence doesn't seem to break any new ground. This is because it was God's plan to change your destination through Christ and then to transform your daily walk by aligning the way you had been thinking with a new thought life. Yes, the changes you make begin by altering the way you think.

If you have been a believer for many years, but still view money the way you always have, how can you expect your financial condition to prosper? The same is true regarding your marriage or relationship. You can be a new Christian and have the same tired marriage. Let me try to say this as simply as I know how: *If you want a new life you have to have a new attitude.*

AN ONGOING PROCESS

With revised thinking you will begin to transform the way you live—and remember, it is an ongoing process, not simply a once-and-for-all decision. I trust you can see the difference in "changing" (continually becoming new) rather than making one change.

This involves constantly taking another look at the way you think about things and seeking what God desires for your thoughts and actions. Otherwise, you will click on "default" and go right back to your familiar behavior.

Growth always results in transformation, so stop resisting. Unless you are God, you have to constantly stay in the mode of becoming new.

With every age and stage of life comes challenges and, hopefully, progress. God is the only one who is perfect, so there is no need for Him to change.

*Jesus Christ is the same
yesterday and today and forever.*
– HEBREWS 13:8 NIV

For I am the Lord, I change not.
– MALACHI 3:6 KJV

We are involved in a special journey, and it entails more than just moving forward on the outside, it's also about development and progress on the inside. So, let's get started.

Regardless of what you desire to see change, the battle will begin in your mind:

- If you think you will always be broke—you will be.
- If you believe you will always be addicted —this will be your fate.
- If you imagine yourself having relationship problems—that will be the outcome.

Things will remain status quo if you never believe they can improve.

Here's how the process works. You have just made a wonderful decision of the heart to make some major changes in your life, but *your mind is going to fight what your heart just decided.*

You may be one of many people who need release from oppressive statements which have been spoken over you in the past. Perhaps you have listened to what others have said about you or their opinion of how you should be living. It could be that your transformation needs to come in the way you think about and handle personal relationships, or maybe it's your physical body that could use a little readjustment.

Most people I meet are caught up in the past with antiquated ideas or concepts that simply are no longer effective. Yet, they refuse to let them go and reach out in faith for something new.

FACE THE FACTS

Here are a few facts you will need to consider when it comes to the changes you are about to make:

Fact #1: Real change begins with a cleaning out process.

It's necessary to discard tired ways of thinking when they don't line up with the direction you are now headed. There has to be some major "cleaning out" before there can be a fresh place for new thoughts to reside.

And no one puts new wine into old wineskins. For the wine would burst the wineskins, and the wine and the skins would both be lost. New wine calls for new wineskins.
– MARK 2:22

Just as Jesus illustrated in the "wineskin" analogy,

you cannot pour new revelations into an old mindset.

LEARNING TO WALK

I heard the plight of a police dog that was injured by an automobile running over its hind legs. After surgery and months of recovery the dog was still unable to use her two back legs. So getting around for this now retired animal was reduced to just dragging her two hind legs behind her while moving forward with her two front legs.

The handicapped dog gave birth to five healthy pups that eventually began to walk by also dragging their two hind legs. After further examination of the puppies it was determined there was nothing wrong with their legs, they were just mimicking their mother!

Be aware of living out issues in the same way your parents did before you. If one of your role models had a negative habit or loved to display plenty of emotional drama, this doesn't mean you also need to be adding chaos to the way you live.

If your parents fought and worried over money, never seeming to have enough, that has nothing to do with your potential for prosperity. Get rid of the idea you have to repeat what you have witnessed or lived out in your past. This is a brand new day and it begins with a spring cleaning of your old way of thinking.

LETTING GO!

I pastor a wonderful congregation in Grand Junction, Colorado. I also do some consulting with other churches that have stagnated when is comes to the issue of numerical growth. One of the challenges that I and the staff of our church face on a regular basis is to motivate people to abandon their preconceived ideas about church. But until I can convince them to let go of their past misconceptions it is difficult to get them to fully embrace the amazing new things God is doing in His church today.

For I am about to do something new.
See, I have already begun! Do you not see it?
– ISAIAH 43:19

Many believers are tragically missing out on what the Lord is waiting to pour into their lives because

47

they are hanging onto traditional methods used in the days of their great, great grandparents. The Lord declares:

"They worship me in vain; their teachings are but rules taught by men. You have let go of the commands of God and are holding on to the traditions of men." And he said to them: "You have a fine way of setting aside the commands of God in order to observe your own traditions!"
– MARK 7:7-9 NIV

Believe me when I tell you the church is only one place where people cling onto past behaviors instead of venturing into something new and exciting.

Fact #2: You will be changing as you are on display.

I wouldn't mind being on public display if I were a perfect finished product, but God is using and refining us all at the same time. This means others are going to weigh in on your decisions, right in the middle of the process. During this time it is vital not to let them keep you restrained or held back by their memory of who you used to be.

Have you ever talked to an old friend who you haven't seen or heard from in ten or fifteen years? It probably won't be long before you realize that after a little reminiscing about days past you may not really know each other anymore. Both of you have significantly changed over the years and you *should* have.

Far too often, the people who are closest to you will fight the steps they see you taking. This is why you need to tell them of the new developments you are experiencing.

Fact #3: You must be free to change.

When people are accusing you of no longer being the same you, try to avoid arguing with them, because denying it makes a negative statement. So the next time someone comments, "Man you have changed," just simply answer by smiling and saying, "Thank You."

Don't let others freeze you in a moment of time and it is equally important that you do not do this to yourself. One way some have remained stagnant is by failing to admit they were wrong in the past. Either out of embarrassment or pride many people will hold onto something they no longer even believe because they lack the courage to admit, "I was wrong."

Have you ever said you didn't like a particular person, only to learn more information about them later which caused you to regret your hasty first impression?

TAKE THE INITIATIVE

We have to stop people from believing that when we are an adult we no longer change or grow. In the sight of God we are a continual work in process—and confessing we were once wrong and expressing our new feelings on the subject should be a common occurrence.

Once you have announced to your family and closest friends that you are ready to make some serious changes, you must take the initiative before anything real or substantive will happen. Those who are waiting on another person in order for their life to be enriched will likely be the same twenty years from now.

Fact #4: You will need some help in order to change.

Everyone needs assistance when the time comes to make changes for the better. Without a helping hand, we can so easily slip right back to the way we used to think, act and talk. It is far too easy to revert into the comfort zones of how we have always done things. God wants to help us in this area.

> *I lift up my eyes to the hills— where does my help come from? My help comes from the Lord, the Maker of heaven and earth. He will not let your foot slip— he who watches over you will not slumber.*
>
> – PSALM 121:1-3 NIV

God loves to partner with you on the things you can't do on your own. Certainly it forms a special bond when someone offers you help and comes through for you in your hour of need. However, there are those who only do this when it is convenient for them. But the Lord's agenda is always focused on you. He is waiting, ready to encourage and help.

God is our refuge and strength,
always ready to help in times of trouble.
— PSALM 46:1

Not only is your heavenly Father wanting to assist you, He also desires to give you direction regarding the areas of your life you need to be re-examining.

Who are those who fear the Lord? He will
show them the path they should choose. They
will live in prosperity, and their children will inherit the
land. The Lord is a friend to those who fear
him. He teaches them his covenant.
— PSALM 25:12-14

BEYOND WISHING AND HOPING

I have seen many who desperately needed to redirect certain aspects of their lives. I have heard them pray, wish and hope for a miraculous transformation to take place. They sincerely long for their marriage to return to one of love and harmony, their children to be happy and serving the Lord, and their joy for living to be more evident and consistent.

But sadly, many will not move forward until the pain of staying where they are is unbearable.

Why wait for the pain and agony? Life renewal begins with a new attitude and a revitalized way of thinking. It may not always be an easy path, but with God's help it will lead to triumph.

CHAPTER FOUR

DESTINY CONNECTIONS

P reviously, I introduced you to the three ingredients which have the potential to shape you into the man or woman God intends for you to be: Change—Construct—Complete.

We learned how our destiny decisions involve being willing to embrace constant change—and the number one area to zoom in on is our attitude.

Before we address the issue of "Construct," I want to first share a major component the Lord will use in your transformation process. It's called a "Destiny Connection."

I am referring to a person or ministry that challenges you to raise your sights and become a better person. This is a connection which inspires, motivates and encourages you to keep growing and moving forward. It is a link which often feels like a loving arm wrapped around you, while at other times resembles the toe of a boot upside your—well you get the picture!

This is a connection with *purpose*. One the Almighty has placed in your path to launch you toward the vision the Lord wants you to enjoy first hand.

When you are in such a relationship, you must protect, nurture and appreciate the potential and value it brings to your life.

One of the ways you will know this is a God-given partnership is that the enemy will try to come against you. Satan knows if he can just get a foot in the door and allow a spirit of disconnection from this person or ministry to creep in, your advancement will be crippled.

THE RIGHT ALLIANCE

We find scores of destiny connections in the Bible. Elisha shared such a bond with Elijah, Ruth with Naomi and Abraham with Sarah.

Even though Sarah was well advanced in years, she was 90, a "nation" was to be birthed from her body in the form of a son named Isaac. Had Abraham not stayed connected with Sarah—for any reason—he would have forfeited his entire purpose for being alive. He would have missed his destiny.

The right alliances are vital to maintain, and the wrong ones need to be relegated to the past. Strange as it seems, inappropriate friendships are usually harder to leave, and the acceptable ones are under constant attack. I wonder who's behind this?

A JEALOUS FATHER

One of the best illustrations of this in Scripture is the story of the relationship between David and Jonathon. Young Jonathon was the son of Saul, the first King of Israel.

Of course David was the one who killed Goliath and was chosen by God to be the next to sit on the throne. David was Jonathon's *God* connection, while Saul was Jonathon's *flesh* connection. And the carnal was in a battle to destroy the divine.

While Jonathon had a virtuous heart, he was

terrible at decision making. And this would eventually cost him his life.

Unfortunately, Jonathon had his father's DNA, but he was different than Saul—especially regarding character and integrity. His desires, values and thinking were totally opposite.

King Saul had grown cruel and abusive. At one point he even tried to murder his son due to his insatiable rage and jealousy of Jonathon's "God association" with David.

> *Saul boiled with rage at Jonathan. "You stupid son of a whore!" he swore at him. "Do you think I don't know that you want him to be king in your place, shaming yourself and your mother? As long as that son of Jesse is alive, you'll never be king. Now go and get him so I can kill him!" "But why should he be put to death?" Jonathan asked his father. "What has he done?" Then Saul hurled his spear at Jonathan, intending to kill him.*
>
> – 1 SAMUEL 20:30-33

As Christ followers, the enemy will always try to

remove these destiny connections from your life—and the number one method Satan uses to accomplish this is through those with whom you are the closest. In far too many cases, dearest friends have no desire to see you advance into the life God has planned. Like Saul, they become jealous.

It might be a family member or a trusted associate who tries to subtly (or not so subtly) encourage you to separate yourself from any influence which is helping to improve your future.

You must be aware of the "Sauls" who seem to treat you with kindness until your plan for following God's leading is revealed.

A COSTLY DECISION

Later in this biblical account, Jonathon meets with David in a field to give warning how Saul is searching for him because he wants to kill him—and that he should run for his life.

Jonathon hugged his dear friend and returned to the palace. This is where Jonathon made a decision which would cost him his future and his very life. He left his "God connection" and turned back in an attempt to repair the damage his bond with David had cost him at home. What a tragic mistake.

Sometimes following God goes against everything the flesh tells you to do, but you must obey the Lord because He has a plan for your life.

Jonathan never wore the robe of a king because he was killed in a battle with the Philistines (1 Samuel 31:2). In the same battle, King Saul was wounded, but he actually died by committing suicide. The Bible says, *"Saul took his own sword and fell on it"* (verse 4).

Immediately, David came out of hiding and was crowned king of Israel.

Had Jonathon stayed with David he could have lived the rest of his life in the palace like a king—without the pressure of the position. But his decision to return to Saul changed everything.

As you read in the Old Testament, the people who remained loyal to David were blessed. Sure there was conflict, yet when the smoke cleared there was glorious victory.

THE PRICE OF SEPARATION

When the Lord leads you into a spiritual alliance,

it is your responsibility to stay connected!

I received a letter from a woman who attended our church many years ago. Then one day something caused her to pull the plug and leave.

She explained in her letter how she and her husband were attending our church and serving in one of our areas of ministry, but after going through a difficulty in their marriage, they decided to leave, rather than keep coming and feeling like hypocrites. As a result, their marriage ended and she soon married another man who did not know the Lord. For the next several years she and her children lived in an abusive household.

Sadly, in her desperate search for escape, she became addicted to drugs.

Now, eleven years later, after finally ending the disastrous relationship, she had the courage to write me. In her letter she described the "sense of belonging" she felt when they were in our church and how she and her children longed for that connection again. She even used the words, "Our life had never been better than the time we spent in Fellowship Church in Grand Junction."

I'm happy to report this single mom and her three children are now attending a wonderful church in another state and being supported and encouraged by family members and those in the congregation. But what a waste of eleven years. And what a tragedy for damage to be inflicted on innocent children along the way.

STAY PLUGGED IN!

Trouble is going to surface whether you are in a good church or not; none of us are immune. However, the last thing you should do when problems arise is to disconnect from your power source. I like to think of the House of God as a sanctuary where you are consistently getting a "trickle charge" to boost your spiritual battery for the rest of the week. You certainly don't want to unplug!

This woman's story is one I have seen repeated countless times. People are active in a fantastic congregation; they are worshiping, giving, serving and changing their lives for the better. Their relationships are blossoming, their attitudes are improving, they are forgiving, controlling their anger issues and making great strides. Then something happens—and who knows why?

This reminds me of what I heard a pastor once say, "If you have not been hurt in church, you simply have not gone long enough!"

I can't begin to count the number of people I've seen walking around our city who were once involved in a church, connected to a pastor who was teaching and helping them and other Christians—then, for whatever reason, they just disconnect.

Friend, your "God partnerships" are both valuable and vulnerable, and they must be nourished and protected. It is also true that every time a person makes the decision to leave, in addition to being a loss for him or her, it is also a heartache for those who love and care for them spiritually.

HURT FEELINGS?

A longtime friend called me recently. He owns a successful company in another state and has been a Christian for over forty years. The man began his conversation by bluntly telling me he was quitting his home church. This single 58-year-old business genius was leaving a congregation he cherished and a pastor and people who loved him, because his feelings were hurt.

He tried to explain how the church was involved in a building program and the outside general contractor the church board hired had overlooked him and his company for one of the sub-contractor positions for the new project. Now, as a result of this oversight, he was making the decision to leave because the pastor didn't rectify the situation. My dear friend's ego was definitely bruised.

I am a longtime counselor with a degree in biblical guidance and counseling, so with all my expertise and the compassion of a pit bull, I asked him, "What are you, a ten year old? You are about to abandon a priceless God connection in your life that is helping you grow, worship and serve—over having your feelings damaged? Have you lost your mind?"

Then I felt led to just unload on him for awhile, telling him a little more inside information about a pastor's life.

THE LIFE OF A PASTOR

If you really want to try and understand the

work load of your pastor, the easiest way for me to explain it is this: Go to your church website and take a long hard look at the myriad of ministries, events and schedules listed. Do you see them all? Your pastor oversees every one of these.

His portfolio includes staffing and training for the purpose of providing quality age-appropriate ministries for each individual who enters the church doors. From the nurseries and children's ministries, to the teenagers and young adults, young married couples to seasoned families, those who have been divorced to senior adults living on fixed incomes and every other person in a variety of stages and ages of life.

From payroll to budgets, from building plans to property development the senior pastor of your church is overseeing it all. Whether hands-on, directly or indirectly, he is totally involved. In addition, he will also spend eight to fifteen hours every week in his study trying to prepare life-giving messages and praying for you and your family. He will fund raise, problem solve and cast the overall vision for the ministry.

He or someone he assigns will meet with attorneys,

accountants and bankers to make sure that all insurance issues, tax questions and protection plans are kept in order. Oh, and by the way, he is also trying to be an attentive husband to a woman he loves, an involved father to his own children, a provider for his family and a man who would just like to have something that resembles a normal life from time to time!

Prayerfully ask yourself: Are you being taught the Word of God? Do you have opportunities where you can serve the Lord? Are you worshiping in the sanctuary? Are you investing into the lives of other Christians? Do you have opportunities to help those in need? If the answer is "Yes," then thank God, grow up and stay right where you are!

Sometimes you just need to "man up," learn to appreciate all the hats your pastor has to wear and pray for him daily.

The last thing you need to do is to leave your church and inflict your "hurt feelings" virus on another congregation.

TOUGHEN UP!

I would love to be a full time "life coach," but most people don't want to pay $140 an hour to be talked to quite so frankly—but this guy was a personal friend and he could take it from me because he knew I loved him and what I was saying was the truth.

Finally, after telling him the last 2%, the man on the phone agreed with me and said, "You're right. Thanks."

Brace yourself! God's people need to toughen up and stop treating the church like it has to be perfect in order for them to remain a member. Especially when just our very presence makes the House of God imperfect!

When the Lord has planted you in the right place, be wary of the enemy trying to win over your mind or emotions by telling you to pull up roots which have been so carefully and prayerfully planted.

Over the years I have seen many good people make bad decisions regarding this matter. In the process I've watched their lives slide backwards. Even more tragic, as is often the case, one bad choice leads to another, and another. And they refuse to return to the fellowship and ministry of a church because of pride.

Destiny connections are God ordained. Protect, respect and treat them as a spiritual treasure. Your heavenly Father has placed specific people in your path for a divine purpose. They are not always perfect, and there will still be battles to fight, obstacles to overcome, pain and disappointment to contend with. But stay united for the cause of Christ.

ONE CHOICE AFFECTS MANY

Jonathon's decision to leave David and return to Saul may have seemed right to him at that moment, but sometimes good sense doesn't add up to a good life!

Take a soul-searching look at the people dearest and nearest to you and decide which alliances are really from God and which ones are not. Now you have a decision to make that will affect not only your life, but theirs.

As you draw closer to the Lord, I pray you will become their destiny connection. But stay united for the cause of Christ and for your protection.

CHAPTER FIVE

CONSTRUCT!

In the three-step formula which will cause any area of your life to improve, the first stepping stone is *Change*—and now we are ready for the second, *Construct!*

When we decide on what needs to be remodeled, we're ready to enter the building mode. We are now committed and prepared to do something positive about the problem, not just talk about it.

What a waste of knowledge not to expand and enlarge on information you have been taught. Today, at this very moment, is the time to take action.

But don't just listen to God's word.
You must do what it says. Otherwise, you
are only fooling yourselves.

– JAMES 1:22

What are you going to build? Your dream. When God gave Joseph a vision of what would eventually take place, he had to "walk out" the dream he was given.

Certainly, the Lord needs to be the architect of your passions and desires, but He expects you to line up your walk with His plan.

Who are those who fear the Lord? He will show them the path they should choose.
— PSALM 25:12

It always amazes me how far too many believers want to stand back and rely on God to do all the work. The Lord, however, desires to be in partnership with you. Let me put it into perceptive. Yes, it is His vision, but He expects you to take hold of it and step into the challenge.

God will always be there to help and strengthen you along the way, however, He will not do the work for you while you sit back and do nothing. Your faith in the Almighty and your personal efforts must team up and work together.

You say you have faith, for you believe that
there is one God. Good for you! Even the demons
believe this, and they tremble in terror. How foolish!
Can't you see that faith without good deeds is useless?
Don't you remember that our ancestor Abraham was
shown to be right with God by his actions when
he offered his son Isaac on the altar? You see,
his faith and his actions worked together.
His actions made his faith complete.

– JAMES 2:19-22

One of my all-time favorite motivational psalms is the very first one, which speaks of the attitude and actions of a man who is blessed:

He is like a tree planted by the streams of water, which
yields its fruit in season and whose lead does not
wither. Whatever he does prospers.

– PSALM 1:3 NIV

Notice, the text states, *"Whatever he does"*—not

whatever he hopes for or wishes would happen.

JUST IMAGINE!

Once God gifts you with a plan and in your mind's eye you can visualize it, you have to take out your tools and begin the building process. If you are having difficulty seeing the finished results, it is likely you will never complete the task.

- Can you picture yourself in a loving relationship?
- Can you see yourself without an ashtray on your beside table?
- Can you visualize yourself with all your bills paid and being financial secure?
- Can you imagine yourself in better physical shape?

What will you be doing in God's Kingdom five years from today? If your mind can't paint the picture with you in the center, it will not happen. Draw a mental blueprint and look it over carefully. Then set the appropriate objectives, establish the time schedule and start construction.

Here is an outline of goals to help you begin:

Relationship Goals

Every new year I sit down with my wife and together we decide where we want our relationship to be at the end of the coming twelve months. We discuss the needs we both have as a man and woman and review how we have been doing in the past.

Because we are both growing and changing, we make sure we are on target with each other and united in our objectives. Since Anna and I love to travel and play golf, we schedule our vacation time and travel plans before anything else gets written on the calendar. We even write in special seminars or focus group sessions to sharpen our skills at being a God-honoring husband and wife.

I'm trying to let you know that just loving each other deeply, believing in the same Lord and serving Him together is not enough; we have to work at our marriage in order for it to remain healthy, happy, harmonious and fun.

Work Related Goals

Prayerfully decide where you want to be in your occupation over the next year—whether you are an employee or run your own business. How can you better represent the Lord in your work environment and give greater purpose to your career?

Physical Goals

You can't give up on this one! Your body is a temple, the dwelling place of the Lord, and how you treat it shows how much you appreciate His gift. What are your health targets, and how will you reach them? Will you sacrifice and do what is necessary to remain healthy and stay in shape?

I'm not talking about nebulous goals. How much do you plan to weigh on a certain date? What will you blood pressure reading be? Make sure you are specific.

Financial Goals

How much debt do you plan to reduce during the coming twelve months—and how much money do you want to keep in savings or invest in the short term?

Anna and I always set a giving goal each year, and this too reflects on how much money we are praying the Lord will bless us with in the coming year.

Spiritual Goals

Even though I listed this objective last, it certainly is not least in importance. Every Christian should desire a continual closer relationship with God, to hunger for His presence and sense His working in a more tangible manner.

HOW TO ATTEND A CHURCH SERVICE

Since you are on a quest for making some worthwhile life-altering decisions, why not decide to change the way you attend church services. On any given date, your preparation time for arriving at the House of God could be as much as two hours. Then, you will spend another hour and a half at church, and an additional thirty minutes talking with friends, leaving the parking lot and driving home.

This is four hours of your day invested in one church service. Since you can't retrieve these hours, why not make the most of them? By comparison, many people will give more time and thought in preparing for a meeting with their boss on Monday than they do meeting with their God on Sunday!

I attend an estimated 150 church services each year, and spend most of my waking hours in actions or thoughts which revolve around church life.

Let me show you how to make a few adjustments in your personal schedule to gain the most benefit from attending a service in your home church.

First: Pray.

Before you ever arrive at the Worship Center, may I suggest you ask God for forgiveness. Make sure there is nothing hidden which can hinder or get in the way of you worshiping the Lord. Ask Him for discernment or understanding of anything He wants to reveal to you which will heighten your walk with Him.

Second: Come with an attitude of appreciation.

Most of the people who are making the service available to you are sincere, God-honoring volunteers.

Working in the children's church, singing on a praise team or greeting you at the door is someone's son or daughter, of whom their parents are extremely proud. Let people know how much you appreciate their service to the Lord and their efforts in making your church a place you love to bring others.

Third: Quickly and fully engage.

Most church services today are only approximately 70 minutes in length. Maximize every moment you are there by entering into the presence of the Lord without hesitation. Give your total attention to worshiping and hearing God's Word.

Fourth: Serve somewhere.

To accommodate a busy world, many churches have more than one weekend service, making it possible for you to attend one gathering and serve in some capacity during another. Your church life will never be what God intends until you find a place to contribute your time and talent—and do so faithfully and enthusiastically.

Fifth: Prepare God's tithes and your offerings in advance—and come ready to give.

The first tenth of everything God blesses you with that week belongs to Him. Above this amount is what you personally decide to contribute. When you are giving back to the Lord during offering time, do so with an attitude of worship, thanking Him for entrusting you with His abundance in the first place.

Sixth: Bring your friends and family with you.

Attending church services is a community event and an opportunity to introduce others to Christ. Always bring your entire family, along with invited co-workers, neighbors and friends.

Seventh: Seek the Father, not a pastor or people.

The Bible tells us where to search—and what we can expect in return:

He is a rewarder of
those who diligently seek Him.
– HEBREWS 11:6 KJV

The word *diligently* means "industriously, meticulously and thoroughly"—and God says if you will just look for Him with this kind of fervor and passion He will reward you. If you were to try to receive a reward which was posted for finding a missing person, you would first have to actually find the individual! However, God says, "I will pay you just for looking!"

When you attend a church service it is not ultimately the pastor, singers or teachers who are going to help you solve all your problems or meet all your needs. The minister will not be driving to your home that evening to listen to your troubles or give you the answers. He is simply a sign post, pointing you to the One who can. Seek God, not man and you will surely receive a glorious reward for your effort.

FOUR ESSENTIALS FOR BUILDING

We've been discussing what it takes to construct

the life God envisions, but in addition to setting goals and receiving the most out of serving the Lord in your church, there are four basic things you need in order to build your dreams effectively:

#1: Tools

Do you have the right equipment to complete the vision God has birthed within your spirit?

To me, information is a vital tool. For example, if your goal is weight loss, you will need the right nutritional and exercise data to reach your objective.

If your purpose is to improve a relationship, you need to find up-to-date materials on conflict resolution and continued romance. If you have been called to be a Bible teacher, in addition to study helps, an audio library of the best communicators would be an effective resource.

#2: Investment

For first-rate construction there is a price to pay —and without investment there will be no return. I remind couples that strengthening their marriage will involve quality time, attention and maybe even some money, but just think of the cost both emotional and financial if your relationship were to fail!

#3: Materials

As with building anything worthwhile, you will need the right equipment to work with. God will always put in your heart or hand whatever is needed to accomplish the vision. If you are struggling or lack the materials for building your dream, then God probably didn't initiate it in the first place. For example, if no honest person in your life thinks you can sing, the Lord likely didn't give you the dream to be a singer.

#4: Energy

You are a danger to yourself and others if you are not up to the task and worn out before you ever begin. You need the vigor and vitality to stay on the wall and keep building the vision. Let me put it in the simplest of terms: As a woman, you can't exchange vows with your husband for better or for worse and then not have the energy to be a wife. Or, you should not give birth to a child, then not have the patience or stamina it takes to raise your son or daughter in the fear and admonition of the Lord.

Energy springs from taking action. If you lack the get-up-and-go to take a walk, the only way you will have the needed strength is to ease out of that sofa and start walking! The same is true in your marriage. If you don't have the passion to improve your relationship, the only way to obtain it is to take action and re-light the fire—the necessary energy will follow.

You probably didn't notice, but there is an acrostic in these basics. Tools, Investment, Materials and Energy spell the crucial word TIME.

It may take days, weeks or even years to complete your dream. So be patient with yourself and stay consistent in your efforts. If anyone wants to know how you are doing, just smile and tell them, "I have a few areas under construction."

With God as your partner, it is an exciting way to live!

CHAPTER SIX

DON'T WASTE A BLESSED LIFE

Have you ever known a person who on the surface appeared to be a much nicer individual before they were blessed? Let me explain.

Perhaps it was a family member, a close friend, or maybe even it is you. At one time, things were not going well, their life seemed to be in a constant state of disarray, but in spite of if all they were humble, kind and appreciative of anything that even resembled a blessing. It's not that they felt they deserved better, however, they hoped, prayed and worked at achieving something more. But, when things in their life changed for the better, the individual changed for the worse!

Now, rather than being appreciative, they grew arrogant and started feeling not only deserving, but worthy of more. Their once contrite and kind attitude had now been replaced by a side of them you haven't seen before, a disposition which resembles a person who does not value what they have been given, or the people who helped them along the way.

They start acting as if they achieved everything by their own ability, without God's help or His answer to their cries when they were hurting. As a result, they lose it all, only to start over as the person you remember who *was* and is now once *again* respectful, compassionate and thankful.

YOU CAN'T LOSE!

For many, being blessed—really blessed—will be a new experience. When you receive this gift, and I believe you will, don't ever relinquish your most valuable personal asset, which is a contrite, grateful heart.

Remember, you are under construction and remodeling the areas of your life you desperately want to see improved. As you begin to build, however, you are about to be blessed. You are partnering with God, fully committed to His promises and being strongly supported by Him. Here are the facts: *If you obey, you can't lose because God cannot lie!*

WILL YOU KEEP THE BLESSING?

There is not a doubt in my mind that as you are changing your patterns of thinking to line it up with God's and busying you hands to accomplishing the assigned construction work, you will succeed. You are about to enter a life more blessed than anything you can ever imagine.

However, before I explain the last principle in getting your life going again, I am asking you to address this question; Once you start experiencing a truly blessed life, will you be able to keep it? Or will you start acting crazy and let it all slip through your fingers? Do you promise not to waste a life of heavenly favor by treating it foolishly?

I know God wants to bless you, for He says:

For it gives your Father great
happiness to give you the Kingdom.

– LUKE 12:32

*The Lord will withhold no good
thing from those who do what is right.*

– PSALM 84:11

PREVENTIVE MAINTENANCE

I am convinced it is not God who is keeping the windows of heaven closed, because once your life operates in tandem with His plans, blessing will *chase* after you.

*And all these <u>blessings shall come</u>
<u>upon you and overtake you</u>, because you
obey the voice of the Lord our God.*

–DEUTERONOMY 28:2 NKJV

I also believe it would be better to never experience God's favor than to have it for a short period only to lose it later. So I want this teaching to be treated as preventive maintenance, and for you to sustain the right attitude once you start living at a higher level with the Lord.

THE TIMID KING

In chapter four we mentioned King Saul in the context of Johathon's relationship with David. But I want you to understand where Saul began. He started out humbly, even a little timid, not feeling as though he deserved or even could do the job as the first king of Israel.

> And finally Saul son of Kish was chosen
> from among them. But when they looked
> for him, he had disappeared! So they asked
> the Lord, "Where is he?" And the Lord replied,
> "He is hiding among the baggage." So they found
> him and brought him out, and he stood head
> and shoulders above anyone else.
>
> – 1 SAMUEL 10:21-23

Saul was about to be introduced, yet he was hiding. Can you imagine if the next president of the United States was to be presented to our nation at the inauguration ceremony when everything came to a screeching halt because he had locked himself in the bathroom?

After Saul was brought out from his hiding place among the luggage and introduced to the people as their king, he returned to his home with a group of good men God had surrounded him with. But there were a few folks in the crowd who bitterly opposed him being their leader.

When Saul returned to his home at
Gibeah, a group of men whose hearts God
had touched went with him. But there were some
scoundrels who complained, "How can this man
save us?" And they scorned him and refused
to bring him gifts. But Saul ignored them.
— 1 SAMUEL 10:26-27

A BETTER IDEA?

Saul chose to ignore those whose attitudes toward him were contrary to what God desired. Any time you are about to be used and blessed by the Lord in a powerful way there will always be people in your life who will be antagonistic to your agenda. Simply disregard them.

King Saul obeyed God and, as a result, the Lord's

favor rested on his life. He became a respected leader, living an abundant life, and when Saul went into battle, he was victorious!

Then one day God called on Saul to completely destroy the entire Amalekite nation who had been bitter enemies of God for a long time. Saul was to march in and obliterate everyone and everything. But Saul had a better idea, he decided to keep the prime livestock for himself and his men and show mercy toward their king.

Saul and his men spared Agag's life and kept the best of the sheep and goats, the cattle, the fat calves, and the lambs—everything, in fact, that appealed to them.

– 1 SAMUEL 15:9

A WARNING FROM THE PROPHET

So the Lord sent Samuel to find Saul and confront him on his acts of disobedience. And when Samuel asked him point blank, Saul lied about what he had done, telling Samuel he *had* followed God's orders.

When Samuel finally found him, Saul greeted
him cheerfully. "May the Lord bless you," he said.
"I have carried out the Lord's command!"
– 1 SAMUEL 15:13

Samuel questioned him concerning the stolen livestock, and Saul decided to concoct a story that sounded religious in order to justify his actions.

"It's true that the army spared the best
of the sheep, goats, and cattle," Saul admitted.
"But they are going to sacrifice them to the Lord your
God. We have destroyed everything else."
Then Samuel said to Saul, "Stop! Listen to
what the Lord told me last night!"
– 1 SAMUEL 15:15-16

"SAY ON"

When Samuel had heard enough, he stopped Saul in mid-sentence and begin to proclaim the message God had sent him to deliver. Now listen carefully to Saul's reply:

And he said unto him, Say on.

— 1 SAMUEL 15:16 KJV

Everything seemed okay to Saul. He had achieved what he thought was victory over the Amalekites and his people were happy with him. You can almost feel an attitude of disrespect surfacing in Saul's response to Samuel: "If God has something to say to me. I suppose I should hear it."

So Samuel said, "When you were little in your own eyes, were you not head of the tribes of Israel? And did not the Lord anoint you king over Israel? Now the Lord sent you on a mission, and said, 'Go, and utterly destroy the sinners, the Amalekites, and fight against them until they are consumed.' Why then did you not obey the voice of the Lord?"

— 1 SAMUEL 15: 17 -19 NKJV

Samuel was reminding him, "There was a time when you would listen. In the beginning you were so grateful for things you didn't deserve that you would

91

gladly do whatever God asked of you—and ignore what others said. But now you have changed. Your life improved, and you got worse!"

Finally Saul confessed to the truth:

> *Then Saul admitted to Samuel, "Yes, I have sinned. I have disobeyed your instructions and the Lord's command, for <u>I was afraid of the people and did what they demanded</u>."*
> – 1 SAMUEL 15:24

WHAT HAPPENED?

Remember the early characteristic of Saul, when he was first crowned King of Israel? He had the ability to listen to the Almighty and block out those who murmured anything contrary to God's design for his life.

What happened to this attitude? Why was it that before he had prestige or power it didn't matter to him what others might say? Was it possible he valued the opinions of his peers for the purpose of being able to keep what God had given him in the first place?

I believe this is exactly what occurred. God and

God alone had blessed Saul—but then he started looking to others to receive their approval to remain in that prized position rather than keeping it private between him and his God.

Samuel tells Saul that his actions and change in attitude toward the Lord was a personal matter, and since he was now more interested in pleasing the people than relying on God for his blessings, the Almighty was going to take it all back. Samuel tells him:

*Rebellion is as sinful as witchcraft,
and stubbornness as bad as worshiping idols.
So because you have rejected the command of
the Lord, he has rejected you as king."*
– 1 SAMUEL 15:23

Do you see how confused Saul's thinking had eventually become? When he heard he was about to lose everything, rather than falling on his face, begging God's forgiveness for his disrespectful behavior, the king was still more concerned with how he would look in the eyes of his people.

93

*Then Saul pleaded again, "I know I have sinned.
But please, <u>at least honor me before the elders of my
people</u> and before Israel by coming back with me
so that I may worship the Lord your God."*
— 1 SAMUEL 15:30

Saul was expressing, "I have disobeyed by trying to please people instead of my God. I looked to those who didn't give me my blessings as if they had the power to help me keep them. I was proud, and cared more how I was viewed by others than I was by God—and now I am suffering the consequences. So would you at least stand by my side in the sanctuary to make it appear that everything is still okay?"

As we learn, Samuel did accompany King Saul to the house of worship with him one last time, and was by his side when Saul killed the king of the Amalekites. The prophet never saw Saul after that incident.

*Samuel never went to meet with Saul again, but
he mourned constantly for him. And the Lord was
sorry he had ever made Saul king of Israel.*
— 1 SAMUEL 15:35

The story does not end here. Saul was about to experience the difference between political power and God's power. He would soon learn that even his influence and acceptance with people was a gift from God Himself, and that it was his heavenly Father who should have received his undivided attention. Saul's "life change" began as a personal matter between him and the Almighty, and it should have remained that way.

The Philistines closed in on Saul and his sons, and they killed three of his sons—Jonathan, Abinadab, and Malkishua. The fighting grew very fierce around Saul, and the Philistine archers caught up with him and wounded him. Saul groaned to his armor bearer, "Take your sword and kill me before these pagan Philistines come to taunt and torture me." But his armor bearer was afraid and would not do it. So Saul took his own sword and fell on it. When his armor bearer realized that Saul was dead, he fell on his own sword and died. So Saul and his three sons died there together bringing his dynasty to an end.

– 1 CHRONICLES 10:2-6

AVOID THE HARD LESSONS

Once God begins to really bless your life, never get the big head and start to think you arrived where you are on your own merit or that you can remain in this elevated position without acknowledging Him.

Saul was in the heat of another fierce battle when he realized his sons were dead and that he himself was not going to make it out alive. As Scripture records, it was at this point Saul took his own life.

In reality, however, his demise began long before the Philistines ever shot an arrow in his direction. The archers had wounded him, but it was not their arrows which killed him—it was the blade of his own sword.

Often, we as believers exert far too much energy talking about the enemy and not enough time dealing with the damage we inflict upon ourselves because of bad decision making. In the end, self-destruction is the result of a wrong attitude.

God raised Saul from obscurity and made him the king over all Israel, and wherever he raised his sword he was victorious. As long as Saul and the Almighty were united in purpose he could not fail—and the same is true for you. If you and your heavenly Father are in like mind regarding marriage, business or life endeavors, you cannot lose. But if the enemy can cause you to become self-absorbed or start taking God for granted, he has already won.

Satan wants you to forget being thankful for what the Lord alone has given you. He knows that when your unity with the Lord is broken, you will become weak, helpless and easily destroyed.

I pray you will be obedient to God's call and, as a result, will avoid the hard lessons King Saul had to experience.

CHAPTER SEVEN

AVOIDING SELF-INFLICTED WOUNDS

Have you ever thought for a moment that the battle you are fighting or the temptation you are facing may have nothing to do with you? You heard me right! Some of the conflicts in which you are engaged are not about you personally: rather the enemy is attempting to bring harm to your children and grandchildren.

When King Saul was attacked, the devil also destroyed his children and everyone else attached to his family with one exception—Mephibosheth, the crippled son of Jonathon.

One thing you must continually remind yourself of

is that when you are in an argument or disagreement with your spouse, it's not just about *you* fighting with your wife or husband; the tense and stressful atmosphere created also affects your impressionable kids who are often damaged in the process.

The war of words is not just over an issue which is causing you to be unhappy or disconnected; it also involves the enemy trying to destroy the unity and support your children are supposed to feel from being raised in a God-designed family. It encompasses more than you making a stupid decision; it is about your children having to live under a curse as a result of your behavior.

This battle is extremely serious and the enemy knows nothing of the "rules of engagement." So we can't afford to just lie down and give up because what's at stake is far more important. We are involved in spiritual warfare for our families.

"BE CAREFUL"

When God generously opens the windows of heaven and pours out His favor, the enemy will try to blast those blessing right out of your life. Because of

Adam's sin, this is the consequence.

The life God wants you to enjoy is the same one the adversary plots to destroy. And when your journey becomes smoother and you find yourself in a blessed place, don't think for a minute things will become easier and there will be no more skirmishes. When God's people begin to think they are indestructible is the moment they become most vulnerable and risk losing it all.

> *These things happened to them as*
> *examples and were written down as*
> *warnings for us, on whom the fulfillment of the*
> *ages has come. So, if you think you are standing*
> *firm, be careful that you don't fall!*
> – 1 CORINTHIANS 10: 11-12

You and I are not exempt from doing unexplainable, "stupid" stuff. I have witnessed many intelligent, seasoned Christians duped by the enemy into actions that in the natural would have never crossed their minds. These are good men and woman whose number one priority was to serve the God who gave them life, and they passionately followed after Him. And God richly rewarded them.

Looking at it from the outside, you would agree that these leaders were living the dream. Their families were blessed, their marriages seemed healthy and their finances were strong and growing stronger.

Although they were being protected, the enemy never took them out of his scope as a target. "So if you think you are standing firm, *be careful*"—don't let down your guard or stop doing what it took to reach this special place.

SELF-INFLICTED WOUNDS TO AVOID

Let me share three injuries we have a tendency to bring on ourselves:

#1: Disobedience

This one should be a "no brainer." We must do what God tells us to because He has our best interest at heart. He has a plan for our future and knows how we are going to get there, but will we listen?

The commandment for King Saul was crystal clear; to "utterly destroy the entire Amalekite nation." But as we have discussed, Saul did *most* of what God had told him, but then inexplicably allowed the king to live and kept the best of their livestock for himself and his people.

It was a swing and a miss—close, but not close enough.

Friend, we can't disobey our way into the promises or blessings of God. We either do what He commands or we walk in disobedience.

"God Tells Me To"

Like millions, I grew up on the pew of a church. I accepted Jesus as my personal Savior when I was twelve and later gave my life to serve Him completely at the age of sixteen. From that time forward I began reading and studying God's Word seriously, and taking evening Bible courses at the age of seventeen.

I longed to know how the Lord wanted me to live the rest of my life. As I studied Scripture, I read passages such as:

Come, everyone! Clap your hands!
Shout to God with joyful praise!
— Psalm 47:1

I thought this verse meant exactly what it said. We were supposed to get excited when we came into the Lord's presence.

Then I turned to Malachi where it said:

"Bring all the tithes into the storehouse so there will be enough food in my Temple. If you do," says the Lord of Heaven's Armies, "I will open the windows of heaven for you. I will pour out a blessing so great you won't have enough room to take it in! Try it! Put me to the test!"

– MALACHI 3:10

I interpreted this to mean we were to actually give ten percent of our income to God at the church where we are members and being fed—and that we were to test Him in this. Then I read:

I will praise you as long as I live, lifting up my hands to you in prayer.

– PSALM 63:4

Lift up holy hands in prayer, and praise the Lord.
– PSALM 134:2

You can see where I would be confused, because I took God's Word literally—that we should really lift up our hands to pray and praise Him. Oh, wait a minute; I'm not confused, this is exactly what Scripture said we are to do.

Forgive me. I'm not trying to be sarcastic in any way, rather to make an important point. When the Lord tells you to do something, then not obeying because of what others may think reminds us of how King Saul got into trouble.

When a person asks me, "Dan, why do you do the things you do?" My answer is simple: "God tells me to."

I'm the child and He is the Father. I don't have to understand or even try to figure out the reason why. If He instructs me to worship, pray or live in a certain way, I just do as He asks. And when I fail to follow His direction, I apologize to Him and try to get back on the proper path as soon as possible.

It's not my intention to make anyone squirm or feel

uncomfortable when they attend our church services, but I would rather a few be a little ill-at-ease than for all of us to be dead wrong.

This leads us to the next self-inflicted wound we see evident in the life of Saul:

#2: Arrogance

When Samuel confronted Saul's actions of disobedience, he also dealt with the king's attitude, remembering the time when it was so different.

Samuel asked him to recall the years when he was insignificant in his own eyes—when he was a man of meekness rather than bursting with pride and haughtiness.

You would be surprised how many people become successful, then lose the very thing that made them so likeable in the first place—a servant's heart.

A sense of entitlement can create arrogance. You come to the conclusion you actually deserve God's abundance. The Lord chose Saul and set him apart for the position of king, created and equipped him to do the job, then made him look good by giving him victory after victory on the field of battle. Soon, however, Saul tried to act as if he was the one needing to be praised.

As God begins to bless you, one of your greatest assets is a submissive spirit. Don't ever stop truly being appreciative for everything the Lord gives you.

The third self-inflected wound revealed in this story is:

#3: Denial

This one baffles me. Saul blatantly denies disobeying God in the first place and then blames the people for making the mistake—implying it was not his fault. A good leader will always be accountable for his or her actions, right or wrong.

If you are a single woman who is looking for a man to marry, choose one who will assume responsibility —a person who will look at you when times are hard and say, "Baby, I got this car stuck on the side of the road and I will get us out of here. We are going to be all right."

Avoid becoming entangled with an individual who is always passing the buck, blaming others for being in the slow lane of life. Find a man who has no problem saying, "I am sorry"—and likewise if you are the wife.

All Saul had to do was admit he was at fault; to turn to God and apologize for his behavior.

THE FORGIVENESS FACTOR

Saul was anointed, gifted, called by and even empowered by God, and his life is a lesson for us all. *If we are not careful our gift will carry us to places where our character can't keep us.*

What eventually led to Saul's death was his own bitterness. It was not so much his actions but his inner man, his attitude, which caused his profound problems.

Saul was replaced by David, whose conduct seemed even worse. David was a voyeur, adulterer and a murderer. He was what in this day and age we would call "a lost cause"—and so were his kids and grandchildren. David had slept with so many woman that when they thought he was at death's door, they placed a young woman in bed with him and when he didn't awaken or stir, they assumed "The king is dead" (1 Kings 1).

Yet, God said David was better than Saul, and

here's the reason why. The Lord was looking at the heart of David even more so than his actions. Saul didn't necessarily have a filthy life, but he did have a filthy spirit. Saul would not repent. The one major quality which distinguished David from Saul was the fact you couldn't fault David when it came to repenting. He would throw himself on the floor and cry out to God:

Have mercy on me, O God, because of your unfailing love. Because of your great compassion, blot out the stain of my sins. Wash me clean from my guilt. Purify me from my sin. For I recognize my rebellion; it haunts me day and night. Against you, and you alone, have I sinned; I have done what is evil in your sight. You will be proved right in what you say, and your judgment against me is just. For I was born a sinner.

– PSALM 51:1-5

For the life of me, I can't figure out why Saul didn't just look up to the heavens and admit, "I'm sorry; I was wrong. Please forgive me."

We serve a merciful God.

RELATIONSHIP REQUIRES REPENTANCE

If you ever plan on having a quality relationship with another human being, you must be quick and sincere in telling that person you are truly sorry and repentant when you stumble and make life's mistakes. Whether it be with a parent, a child, spouse, a boss or especially your God, there is no relationship without repentance.

It's not always what the enemy can do to harm you that's the problem. It is what you might do personally with self-inflected wounds.

God truly desires to empower, encourage and establish your life. Just remember that when He does, do not lose the very thing that made you so attractive to Him in the first place—a humble and appreciative spirit.

CHAPTER EIGHT

COMPLETE!

I have been giving you a formula based on scriptural principles to apply to any area of your life you desire to see improved. It is made up of three simple words and applications.

The first, *Change!*—you must have a new mind before you can enjoy a new life. This means discarding your old way of thinking. It begins with your thought life and only God can help you make this total transformation.

The second, *Constuct!* This is when you start to build or work on the changes you have prayed and decided upon. You take the initiative and put your hand to the task. Many people are waiting on the Lord when God is actually waiting on them!

Now comes the final ingredient—*Complete!* You

have to finish what you started. Whether it is a house, an exercise program or the parenting process, more than taking the initial step is required. There comes a time when you need to say, "It's done!"

Any couple can repeat the words "I do" at the altar, however, it requires a loving committed husband and wife to celebrate a 50th wedding anniversary and beyond.

FINISH WELL!

It is dangerous to develop the habit of throwing in the towel at the least provocation—and only God can deliver His children from the desire to quit:

I will heal their backsliding.
– HOSEA 14:4 KJV

The Lord desires to heal you from continually walking off jobs, leaving churches, turning away from relationships rather than working on them, or divorcing over trivial matters. Some people accept defeat far too quickly. Finishing well is an essential objective to accomplish in the quest for living the life God intends.

You can't be a person who gives up on people or projects easily and attain anything worth having in the long run. Whatever you start, make sure you have the determination to complete.

FINISH IT!

You probably picked up this book because when you read the title you knew there were certain areas in your walk where you felt at a crossroads. The thought of making better decisions motivated you to get to this point in your reading. So please do not close the pages now.

Finish what you start! Not just the book, but the project—and you are the project. Yes, you are working on *you*.

So how can you accomplish this?

One: Finish In Phases

Anytime you are involved in a major undertaking, it is wise to complete it in a series of small, achievable steps. And there is a satisfaction which is derived from celebrating each phase on your way to your final goal.

When David took out Goliath, he first had to

confront him, then he attacked, next he knock him down before finally slaying the giant with Goliath's own sword.

Is there an overwhelming task looming on your horizon? Instead of trying to accomplish it all with one major action, slow down. Tackle one part of the problem at a time.

Read the first book of the Bible and you'll discover that when God created the world He did so in five phases. After the achievements of each day, He would pause and declare, "It was good."

God rejoiced with each phase, even though He knew there was still more on the agenda.

You and I must also learn to do the same—especially when it comes to the larger endeavors in life. We are not always going to reach our destination in one working day, so we need to fix our sight on the short term goal and rejoice in our progress all along the way.

TAKE TIME TO CELEBRATE!

If you are trying to lose 100 pounds, you might want to throw yourself a little party to celebrate losing every ten—just don't do it with cheesecake and chocolate ice cream!

It also helps to have other people in our lives who can encourage and rejoice with us in the completion of a phase—someone who knows exactly what we are going for and can recognize and acknowledge the success we are making.

It is a very smart woman who can perceive when her husband is attempting to make personal changes to better their relationship and will verbally compliment the effort he has made, rather than constantly reminding him of how far he still has to go!

Let me ask: Are you where you want to be in every area of your life? Perhaps I should change that to: Well, are you at least a little better today than you were one year ago?

If your answer to the last question is "Yes," you should be proud of your accomplishments.

Two: Finish Your Course

The apostle Paul tells us:

> *I have fought a good fight, I have finished my course, I have kept the faith.*
>
> – 2 TIMOTHY 4:7 KJV

You can't run someone else's race; you have to complete your own. This is why it is wrong for you to compare yourself with others or try to equate your life to how another person chooses to live.

When they measure themselves by themselves and compare themselves with themselves, they are not wise.
– 2 CORINTHIANS 10:12 NIV

Instead of constant comparing, make it your aim to be settled on the fact God made you for a purpose —then concentrate on completing the mission.

No matter how well intentioned, people can't supply everything you need. God is the only "All Sufficient One." Everyone else has only part of the answer, which means they are *insufficient.* We must stop looking to others to give us what only the Lord can provide, which is His direction and purpose.

Who are those who fear the Lord? He will show them the path they should choose.

*They will live in prosperity, and their children will
inherit the land. The Lord is a friend to those who fear
him. He teaches them his covenant.*

— PSALM 25:12-14

An ongoing daily relationship with Christ is vital as
it is your lifeline to receiving directions from on high.
Only then will you have the power, provision and
protection you need to not only survive, but succeed.

*There is no one like the God of Israel.
He rides across the heavens to help you,
across the skies in majestic splendor. The
eternal God is your refuge, and his everlasting
arms are under you. He drives out the enemy
before you; he cries out, 'Destroy them!'...He is
our protecting shield and your triumphant
word! Your enemies will cringe before you,
and you will stomp on their backs!"*

— DEUTERONOMY 33:26-27,29

Your heavenly Father does not play games when it
comes to dealing with the obstacles rising against you

as His child. God will give you not only protection, but the strength you need for the days ahead.

You can complete this task because the Lord will give you the ability to confront and triumph over whatever you are facing. For example, if you were to receive bad news tomorrow morning, the Lord will provide you with the capacity to cope with the situation. Whatever you come against, your loving, all-powerful, all-sufficient Father will give you what you need to handle the matter.

DEFY THE ODDS

One of the most difficult things you will ever do is to complete what you begin. The enemy didn't really try too hard to prevent you from starting your relationship with Christ, joining a church or even beginning to serve your heavenly Father. Why? Because he has seen millions start and never finish. The odds are in his favor!

Another reason completing a task is so difficult is because life gets tougher as you get older. You would think that as you age, the journey would become easier due to your experience and added wisdom, yet the truth is that the issues you will deal with are just becoming more complex. You will always require God's assistance and will never grow out of the need for Him.

Three: Finish Well by Pouring Into the Next Generation

You will be able to see further than your days will allow you to go. Your dreams and desires will reach beyond where your body will be capable of taking you—and this is a plus, not a minus. It is also why you can't really finish well unless you are investing in the next generation which is quickly coming behind you.

When I visit a church where there are only are few young couples with growing families and the average age of the attendee is sixty and above, it causes my heart to be a little sad.

These godly people have so much to offer and share with the next generation, so much knowledge they could impart and life stories which could inspire young lives.

God's Word tells us there is nothing new under heaven. Each generation faces the same issues as the one before them. If we are not passing down our experiences and knowledge, we are not fulfilling our mission as the Lord intends. We are instructed to hand down God's truths and not keep them concealed.

We will not hide these truths from our children; we will tell the next generation about the glorious deeds of the Lord, about his power and his mighty wonders.

– PSALM 78:4

What is happening now has happened before, and what will happen in the future has happened before, because <u>God makes the same things happen over and over again.</u>

– ECCLESIASTES 3:15

YOU ARE THE EXAMPLE

The most significant investment you will ever make is to pour your life into the ones who will carry on the work of God long after you leave this earth—those who are trying to build a strong marriage and raise their children in the house of God. They do not need our criticism or even a great deal of coaching. What they hunger for is your encouragement, to see your godly example and be inspired by your resilience, endurance and tenacity. They are going to face exactly the same things we did in our marriages, business, finances and friendships.

Yes, there will be cultural differences, but the major bumps on the road of life will always be the same. The Lord wants us to tell the next generation about the awesome power of God which is available to them, and that He has and *does* still work miracles on behalf of His children.

I have pastored the same church since I was thirty years old. In the process, I have made many mistakes and have even been sidetracked a time or two. My family and church have seen me knocked down only to stand back up and get going again by the grace and power of God, They have heard me tell the Lord, "I am sorry," then return to what He called me to accomplish.

However, what they have never seen—and I pray never will—is for me to give up and quit, for I have a heavenly assignment. When God started His work in me, He promised to finish it.

*Because of your partnership in the gospel
from the first day until now, being confident of this,
that he who began a good work in you will <u>carry it on
to completion</u> until the day of Christ Jesus.*

Every child of God who is over the age of forty should already have a succession plan in place. We should have a certain someone to whom we are pouring in our experiences and knowledge; a person to carry on the vision God has placed in us. This is imperative because the task is not yet finished.

Who are you cheering on and encouraging along the way? Make sure you are investing into the lives of others by letting them hear and see what an awesome God has done in you.

NEVER, NEVER QUIT!

After you begin to make some major life transformations by changing the way you think and you begin the construction project on yourself, there will be times when you may want to slip back to the place were you started, but don't yield to the temptation.

There are many who are watching you, and some are from the next generation. Without question, they will see you fail from time to time and there may even be parts of your life when you don't act as if you belong to God. They will observe you being betrayed, hurting, lonely and even flat out wrong now and then.

Thankfully, they will also be watching as you worship, forgive and ask others to pardon you. But I pray there will be one thing they never see you do—may they never see you quit!

CHAPTER NINE

GOD NEVER MEANT FOR YOU TO LOSE

O utside of God himself, the second greatest and most remarkable power in the world is that of decision making. The ability of a person being able to choose and affect their eternal destiny is a direct result of our being created in the image of the Almighty.

You are an amazing being, because an unbelievable gift has been given to you, and you hold this power in your hands every day of your life.

The decisions you make pave the path to your destiny—where you will eventually be residing. And your choices determine the route you will take to get there. If the options you take don't start working in conjunction with your desired destiny, you will spend your days going around in circles, frustrated, complaining and confused.

God entrusted you with this power of decision making for two reasons:

- First: He really loves and wants you to choose to love Him in return. The Lord doesn't just want computer-chip robots that have no soul or the ability to decide for themselves.
- Second: God trusts you, His child, to make the right decisions, the kind which will align your life with His ongoing plan for you to succeed and thrive.

The Lord commanded us to obey all these decrees and to fear the Lord our God, so that we might always prosper and be kept alive, as is the case today.
— DEUTERONOMY 6:24 NIV

I'm not a fan of the "win some, lose some" philosophy. Instead, I like the idea of *always* winning, *always* advancing and *always* coming out on top.

However, this doesn't mean we won't get knocked down or hurt from time to time. But the idea of "no matter how things look right now if we just stay with God's plan we will triumph" is a very exciting way to live.

AN EMBARRASSING DAY

I took Anna to an NFL Football game in October, 2007. The Bronco's were playing the San Diego Chargers in Denver.

It started out as a perfect fall afternoon and the stadium was packed with enthusiastic fans who were anticipating a victory over the league rival. Within the first five minutes the Chargers had scored two touchdowns and the perfect fall day was starting to feel cold and wet. As the weather turned sour so did the score and before it was all over the Bronco's were handed their worst home game loss in their franchise history, 41 to 3.

Denver had won a couple of games prior to this, so the overwhelming defeat came as quite a shock. After the game, coach Mike Shanahan was quoted as saying, "I don't think our players have ever been more embarrassed."

An attitude of wining on one day and losing on another is the expected norm for most people, but not for God. There is no record in history where you find the Lord has ever lost or failed. He has never even been behind a quarter or two and found it necessary to catch back up for the victory! He has always overwhelmed and defeated His opponents, whether in the spiritual or physical realm. He is God—and He does not lose!

FAILURE IS NOT AN OPTION

If you and I are created in the image of the Almighty and we belong to His family because we have asked Jesus to be our Savior, aren't we also supposed to win? I don't mind taking a few hits for the team from time to time, and I expect to be bruised or roughed up as part of the conflict, but I also expect to raise my hands in victory when the final whistle is blown.

God didn't send His Son to die and conquer death, hell and the grave so you could go through life as a loser. No matter what giant rises against you, failure is not an option. Being defeated, stuck in the same place and miserable are not the plans your loving, all-powerful Father has in mind.

It's time to get the expectation of winning infused into your spirit. Even if in the past you have been slammed to the ground and hurt, this doesn't have to become a life pattern. It is not God's will for you to remain trapped by a problem that is defeating you. You are to be a conqueror and forge ahead.

The righteous keep moving forward,
and those with clean hands become
stronger and stronger.
– JOB 17:9

God created us to be an ever-advancing people who are living by faith, not just repeating the same mistakes we have made in the past.

"DON'T STOP PLEADING"

New obstacles will arise which require an ongoing walk with God and continual power and protection from Him. When you are in "right standing" with the Lord, you are absolutely going to move ahead. However, the key to pressing onward is your personal relationship with God.

This is what we see in Old Testament battles. For example:

When the Philistine rulers heard that Israel had gathered at Mizpah, they mobilized their army and advanced. The Israelites were badly frightened when they learned that the Philistines were approaching.

– 1 SAMUEL 7:7

In this account we read how much the children of God were trembling in fear when they knew the enemy forces were quickly advancing toward them. Not one drop of blood had been shed, yet they were immobilized by what was taking place in their own minds—and this is where almost every true battle begins.

"Don't stop pleading with the Lord our God to save us from the Philistines!" they begged Samuel.

– 1 SAMUEL 7:8

I love those words, "Don't stop pleading," because

no matter how ominous things appear or how outnumbered or outsmarted we are in a specific circumstance, the situation is not over if we continually remember the "God Factor." I'm talking about factoring the Lord into the problem.

When God performs His work, it doesn't matter what the report looks like, what the doctor says, or how downcast you may feel. Your heavenly Father's involvement changes everything!

ARE YOU BOTHERING GOD?

I was speaking with a gentleman after church one Sunday morning and he told me, "I only ask God one time for something; after that I just drop it, I don't want to bother Him."

Not me! I will ask, then keep presenting my need to Him again and again until I receive the answer. I want the Lord to know I am serious and how important this request is to me. I am not shy or reluctant to tell Him, "Lord, I really need Your involvement with this one."

God and I are doing life together and I am in constant need of His help.

STAY CLOSE

To paint a picture, let's imagine you want to build your dream house on a piece of property you own and you also have in mind the perfect contractor to be the builder. Would you just walk by him on the street one day and casually comment, "Hey man, my wife and I want you to build a house for us"—and say nothing else? Would there be no further conversation, no additional details or input and no other planning meetings together? Of course, not. If you desire to tackle such a project you would stay in close communication until the plans were drawn and every last specific detail was settled.

So why do we think it's okay to carry on long, detailed conversations over building a home, yet only have time to send up a one-time request to our God when it comes to much more serious life issues?

"LORD, HELP US!"

We are in a relationship and a partnership with the Lord and He deserves an ongoing interchange when it comes to what is important. Keep asking and talking to God about the matter until every last detail is accomplished. Never stop pleading!

> *So Samuel took a young lamb and offered it to the Lord as a whole burnt offering. He <u>pleaded with the Lord to help</u> Israel, and the Lord answered him.*
> *– 1 SAMUEL 7:9*

What was their cry when God's children knew they were in trouble? It was, "Lord, help us." Just as in the days of old, there are so many areas in our lives where we need God's assistance:

- "Please help me be a good husband."
- "Please help me to financial provide for my family."
- "Please help me repair a broken relationship."
- "Please protect my children."

There is nothing or no one we can't bring before the Lord.

In the above passage, before pleading with God for assistance, Samuel brought an offering to the Lord. He returned a portion of what the Almighty had already given him in the past. His sacrifice was an acknowledgment and "Thank You" for what happened yesterday before he made an additional request. It's a practice we all should follow.

Just as Samuel was sacrificing the burnt offering, the Philistines arrived to attack Israel. But the Lord spoke with a mighty voice of thunder from heaven that day, and the Philistines were thrown into such confusion that the Israelites defeated them.

– 1 SAMUEL 7:10

This is a perfect example of the "God Factor" we mentioned earlier. The Lord, speaking with the crashing sound of thunder, frightened the enemy into a state of total disarray and helplessness. The invading army wasn't just disoriented, they were defeated! What seemed to be an impossible situation for the children of Israel was turned around when God showed Himself in power.

YOU'RE EMPOWERED TO HELP

No matter what you are facing today, begin by

asking God to help you and keep knocking on His
door. Then watch as whatever is coming against you
turns and runs.

The men of Israel chased them
from Mizpah to a place below Beth-car,
slaughtering them all along the way.

– 1 SAMUEL 7:11

This detail is important. The Almighty shows up,
the enemy flees—and God's children chase them!

Notice, the Israelites still had to do their part in
obtaining the complete victory. They had to exert
their energy and take action in this partnership with
the Lord in order to achieve their goals.

This is the way God plans it. He wants to help you,
and you may be aware the Lord is watching over you,
but do you recognize the fact He is also empowering
you?

Samuel then took a large stone and
placed it between the towns of Mizpah and
Jeshanah. He named it Ebenezer (which means

*"the stone of help"), for he said, "Up to
this point the Lord has helped us!"*

– 1 SAMUEL 7:12

By using the words "Up to this point," Samuel was reminding the Lord, "We have a history together. I get myself in trouble; I ask for Your divine help and You answer."

What an amazing, loving, forgiving and powerful God we serve.

Personally, my journey with the Lord gives me confidence He can and *will* do it again. I'm talking about His "God Stuff"—His taking action and offering me help when I ask.

Sometimes I smile and tell God, "I can't do this on my own, and since we are in this thing together, would You show off a little? Remind the enemy Who I love, Who I serve and why I'm still standing—just show them YOU!"

RESCUE AND REFUGE

Samuel was a man of prayer, and the one thing the adversary doesn't want to see is you on your knees.

The devil doesn't mind you complaining or dialing 1-800-CRY-BABY, but it upsets him when you start calling on the name of the Lord.

If I start pleading with God to help me, He will turn over tables and shake the walls if this is what it takes to bring His support to my side.

> *I am praying to you because I know you*
> *will answer, O God. Bend down and listen as I*
> *pray. Show me your unfailing love in wonderful ways.*
> *By your mighty power you rescue those*
> *who seek refuge from their enemies.*
> – PSALM 17:6-7

Prayer is not an activity in futility, rather it is you in fellowship and communion with your Father in heaven:

- No one has ever had your best interest at heart as He does.
- No one has ever loved you like the Lord.
- No one has ever thought about you as often as your heavenly Father.
- No one can rescue you and turn your world around as quickly and thoroughly as God

can—and He will do just that if you ask Him.

Yes, there will be times when you feel defeated, disappointed and discouraged; there will be days when the reports you are hearing cause your mind to imagine the worst.

This is when you must stop and make a truly vital decision—factoring God into the equation.

Your choice will bring results beyond belief, because you are designed and empowered to win.

CHAPTER TEN

DON'T STOP LIVING!

I t probably won't be long after you finish this book or hand it to a friend that unseen forces will attempt to stop you from continuing the process of making destiny decisions. I know this is true, because whether you like it or not you are in a struggle right now.

You have an enemy who despises you, and he not only wants to destroy your life, he is looking for ways to damage your family as well. You probably won't see him coming unless you are paying real close attention to your thoughts, for Satan's attack is not likely to arrive in your front yard as flesh and blood. He wages war against your mind.

One of his strategies is to tell you God isn't paying attention and where you are today is where you will always be. He will whisper, "You've tried this before and you are right back where you started."

If you are not careful you will stop living. Yes, you will still be walking around, breathing and going to work, but not really progressing the way God intends.

This is why I pray you will use the principles of this book again and again to keep your thoughts and actions headed in the right direction.

A SATISFYING LIFE

The Evil One will do his best to rob you of the joy God has in mind for you—including killing your hopes and shattering your dreams for the future. But Jesus is waiting to give you a life that is truly extraordinary.

The thief's purpose is to steal and kill and destroy. My purpose [Jesus] is to give them a rich and satisfying life.
– JOHN 10:10

The closer you move toward the Lord the more your enemy will fight—and your flesh will be of no help either. Your carnal man will always pull you back toward the place where you have been most comfortable in the past.

If you have been in an abusive relationship, as you try to escape, there will be a period between where you were and where you are going that feels uncertain. This is when your flesh will try to yank you back to where you started, your default zone.

When you are in a crisis, it is natural to be afraid, but never give up. If you do, you'll be sending yourself to the end of the line and have to go through the process all over again. If you are recovering from an addiction, you may need to make a destiny decision every day for the rest of your life, but decide with God's help to go for it. Choose to live!

Today I have given you the choice between life and death, between blessings and curses. Now I call on heaven and earth to witness the choice you make. Oh, that you would choose life, so that you and your descendants might live! You can make this choice by loving the Lord your God, obeying him, and committing yourself firmly to him. This is the key to your life. And if you love and obey the Lord, you

will live long in the land the Lord swore to give your
ancestors Abraham, Isaac, and Jacob."
– DEUTERONOMY 30:19-20

The key to a fulfilling life is to decide to love and obey the Lord your God and to commit yourself totally to Him. This is what unlocks the door to the Father's unmerited favor—and it's the foremost choice you will ever make.

THREE CHOICES

Let me give you a few additional life-altering decisions that can be used as weapons in your arsenal and move your life forward. They are choices you will need to make daily:

One: "I will overcome setbacks."

The book of Joshua is the account of an exciting adventure taken by God's people which advanced them to a blessed place prepared by the Lord.

Joshua was an aggressive leader who would do anything the Lord asked him to. Yet, in a situation where God gave the orders and he stepped forward, he suffered a setback. We read:

142

But Israel violated the instructions
about the things set apart for the Lord.
A man named Achan had stolen some of
these dedicated things, so the Lord was very
angry with the Israelites. Achan was the son of
Carmi, a descendant of Zimri son of Zerah, of the tribe
of Judah. Joshua sent some of his men from Jericho
to spy out the town of Ai, east of Bethel, near Beth-
aven. When they returned, they told Joshua, "There's
no need for all of us to go up there; it won't take more
than two or three thousand men to attack Ai. Since
there are so few of them, don't make
all our people struggle to go up there."

– JOSHUA 7:1-3

So approximately 3,000 warriors were
sent, but they were soundly defeated. The
men of Ai chased the Israelites from the town
gate as far as the quarries, and they killed about thirty-
six who were retreating down the slope. The Israelites
were paralyzed with fear at this turn of events, and
their courage melted away. Joshua and the elders of

143

*Israel tore their clothing in dismay, threw dust on
their heads, and bowed face down to the ground
before the Ark of the Lord until evening.*

– JOSHUA 7:4-6

Before the children of Israel were engaged in the battle of Ai, they had destroyed the city of Jericho.

Even though they had not had a real "pay day" for forty years, in the battle of Jericho, God wanted them to exercise their trust in Him by destroying everything within its walls. This was to be their "first fruit" city where the Lord asked them to give all they took back to Him as an offering.

This is exactly what Joshua's armies did, except for one man by the name of Achan, who stole certain items set aside for the Lord.

Next they came to the city of Ai and sent out some battle commanders to decide on a strategy. As we see in God's Word, one battle will usually lead to another and success always includes a plan.

However, the Israelite soldiers lost this confrontation and Joshua could not believe the outcome. This wasn't supposed to happen. They didn't wage the war to lose and suffer casualties. So Joshua tore his cloths and fell on the ground and asked God why. As Scripture records:

Then Joshua cried out, "Oh, Sovereign Lord, why did you bring us across the Jordan River if you are going to let the Amorites kill us? If only we had been content to stay on the other side!

— JOSHUA 7:7

Notice Joshua's thinking process when this setback hit them, "I only wish we would have stayed where we were." If we aren't careful, this is how the enemy will cause us to think. "Things really weren't as bad as we thought they were. Maybe we shouldn't be trying to forge ahead so quickly."

Before the Lord speaks up, Joshua tries to explain to God how this defeat is going to bring dishonor to His name:

"Lord, what can I say now that Israel has fled from its enemies? For when the Canaanites and all the other people living in

*the land hear about it, they will surround us and
wipe our name off the face of the earth. And then
what will happen to the honor of your great name?"
But the Lord said to Joshua, "Get up! Why are you
lying on your face like this? Israel has sinned and
broken my covenant! They have stolen some of the
things that I commanded must be set apart for me. And
they have not only stolen them but have lied about it
and hidden the things among their own belongings.
That is why the Israelites are running
from their enemies in defeat. For now Israel itself
has been set apart for destruction. I will not remain
with you any longer unless you destroy the things
among you that were set apart for destruction."*

– JOSHUA 7:8-12

There was just one solitary man in the entire camp
who did not follow God's orders concerning Jericho
being the "tithe city"—and now the whole army of
God's people were paying the price for his sin.   This
is an example which shows us it *does* matter who we
connect ourselves with.

I recently heard about an answering machine

message that went something like this, "I am not available right now, but thank you for calling. I am making some changes in my life. Please leave your name and number and a brief message after the beep. If I do not return your call, you are one of those changes!"

"GET UP!"

Achan was about to be one of the changes in Joshua's life and God had to give him a defeat in order to identify who was not really with Joshua in the first place. Once this was brought to light, he could proceed into the future without the sabotage of someone close to him.

"Get up! Command the people to purify themselves in preparation for tomorrow. For this is what the Lord, the God of Israel, says: Hidden among you, O Israel, are things set apart for the Lord. You will never defeat your enemies until you remove these things from among you.

— JOSHUA 7:13

I love the fact Joshua was in a genuine relationship with God and not just caught up in religious ceremony. He would argue with the Lord, try to plead his case and reason; then God would reveal some detail Joshua had not known before and would tell him to "Get up" and get back on the saddle again. And this is exactly what Joshua did.

This sounds to me like a strong relationship, one that is built on trust, love and honesty.

Joshua corrected the problem and banished Achan from the camp. Only then was he able to lead Israel against Ai for the second time—and they were victorious (Joshua 8).

This was not Joshua's final battle, nor his last victory. It demonstrates the necessity of having a partnership with God because you will need someone to talk and counsel with along the way; a person who will be your source for wisdom, strength, who will talk you out of quitting and will give you the stamina to stay in the fight.

Setbacks are setups for increase. Before you can have any real measure of growth, it will almost always be preceded by some level of reverse.

Two: "I will fight to keep a good attitude."

In one seminar, I asked a group of successful church staff pastors this question: "How essential is having a good attitude when it comes to being successful in any area of life?"

Without exception, they all agreed that after spending time with God in prayer and reading the Word, their outlook was the single most important decision they would make on a daily basis to give them the ability to do their work efficiently.

Controlling their attitude was one of their highest priorities. One pastor commented, "Every person I know with a good attitude has fought for it."

This is so true. People are not just born with positive outlooks, they have to take specific actions to make sure they remain confident and optimistic.

So I asked what they did during any given day to keep their spirit in an affirmative, enthusiastic mode. Here were their answers:

"I give myself a 'time out.'"

One staff member stated, "I have found that I can't make attitude adjustments on the fly. I don't need a day or even an hour, but I do take about ten minutes or so to ask myself what is happening and why I'm responding like this. Then I decide I don't want to be the kind of person I was seeing in myself, so I change, go back out and face the world."

Taking this "time out" goes right along with what God says:

Be still, and know that I am God!

– PSALM 46:10

In quietness and trust is your strength.

– ISAIAH 30:15 NIV

You don't just stop and take a moment because you are weak; you do so because of your need to become stronger.

"I pray."

Another staff pastor told me, "When I see my

attitude is being challenged and I feel it slipping south I will usually say something to the Lord like this: "God, this is a problem I need to talk to You about. I am so afraid that I am not going to handle this correctly and end up hurting someone." Then he continued, "I will usually pray a few Scriptures such as":

Do not let any unwholesome talk come out of your mouth....Be kind and compassionate to one another.
— EPHESIANS 4:29, 32 NIV

"I listen to spirit-lifting music."

One participant commented, "I either have a CD in my car or an iPod full of inspiring praise and worship music. No matter what I'm facing that is challenging my outlook, I have found uplifting, worship-centered music turns my thoughts around quickly."

"I work out or exercise."

The next staff member said, "Just taking a walk or going on a bike ride will help me get my attitude back on track. There is a definite connection between our physical and emotional well being. I have found that working on my physical health is an automatic for my emotional health and thinking."

"I rest."

One staff member told us she had preschoolers and that they weren't the only ones who needed to take a nap from time to time!. "If it's just a ten to fifteen minute power nap, it does wonders for my attitude."

Note: Jesus would guide His disciples on this matter by making sure they had plenty of rest before dealing with people. At times He would send them up a mountain to camp and rest before heading into another town to witness and minister.

Have you ever noticed that it is usually at the end of a busy day when you tend to be more anxious and worried over things than in the morning after a good night's rest?

"I call a few close life-giving friends."

This one really works for me and it is exactly what the Great Physician ordered:

*And all the believers met together in one
place... They worshiped together at the Temple
each day, met in homes for the Lord's Supper, and
shared their meals with great joy and generosity
—all the while praising God and enjoying
the goodwill of all the people.*
— ACTS 2:44, 46-47

There is a distinct difference between life-giving friends and those who are life-draining. You have to be around both of them from time to time, but when your attitude needs to be boosted, skip the "drainers" for awhile and get around those who can make you smile.

Three: "I will hold onto God's best."

I wish I would have learned the *80/20 Life Satisfaction Principle* many years ago. Nothing in this world will give you 100% of what you want. Nothing human, tangible or touchable; not a parent, child, job, wife, husband or even a church. And the problem with not receiving 100% is that after you get used to the

80%, the enemy will cause the 20% you are *not* getting to look bigger than the 80% you already have!

Many good churches have been left because of the 20% people felt they weren't getting. Many good women have been left for the 20% a man felt was more important. The problem always arises when you finally wake up with the "20" and realize you gave up the "80" to have it.

REVELATION DECISIONS

Throughout this book I have emphasized that great decisions lead to a great life.

Some of these are *revelation* decisions—ones tied directly to your destiny. These come straight from God Himself.

But it was to us that God revealed these things by his Spirit. For his Spirit searches out everything and shows us even <u>God's deep secrets</u>. No one can know a person's thoughts except that person's own spirit, and no one can know God's thoughts except God's own Spirit. And we have received God's Spirit (not the world's spirit), so we can know

the wonderful things God has freely given us.
– 1 CORINTHIANS 2:10-12

My decision to marry my high school sweetheart over thirty years ago was a destiny decision, a connection God would use to help move me forward and fill my life with laughter and love along the journey.

The decision I made to pastor a Church in Grand Junction, Colorado, was also a destiny decision and I would not be who I am today without my wife, Anna, or the wonderful people of Fellowship Church.

When your story is written, which of your choices will be the major turning points?

YOU HAVE THE ANSWERS

I am reminded of a six year old boy and his pet cat who, just a few days earlier, had given birth to a litter of kittens. He came into the kitchen and excitedly announced to his mother, "We have two boy and two girl kittens."

Curious, the Mom asked her son, "How do you know there are two boys and two girls?"

The little boy replied, "I saw Dad pick them up and

look underneath—it must be printed somewhere on the bottom!"

Yes, the answers you are looking for are printed somewhere. I pray you have found them on the pages of this book and, with God's direction, they will be a continual source of guidance and encouragement.

Be blessed!

NOTES

FOR A COMPLETE LIST
OF PUBLICATIONS AND MEDIA MATERIALS,
OR TO SCHEDULE THE AUTHOR FOR
SPEAKING OR CONSULTING ENGAGEMENTS,
CONTACT:

DAN HOOPER
HOOPER MINISTRIES
765 24 ROAD
GRAND JUNCTION, CO 81505

www.hooperministries.com
www.fellowshipgj.com